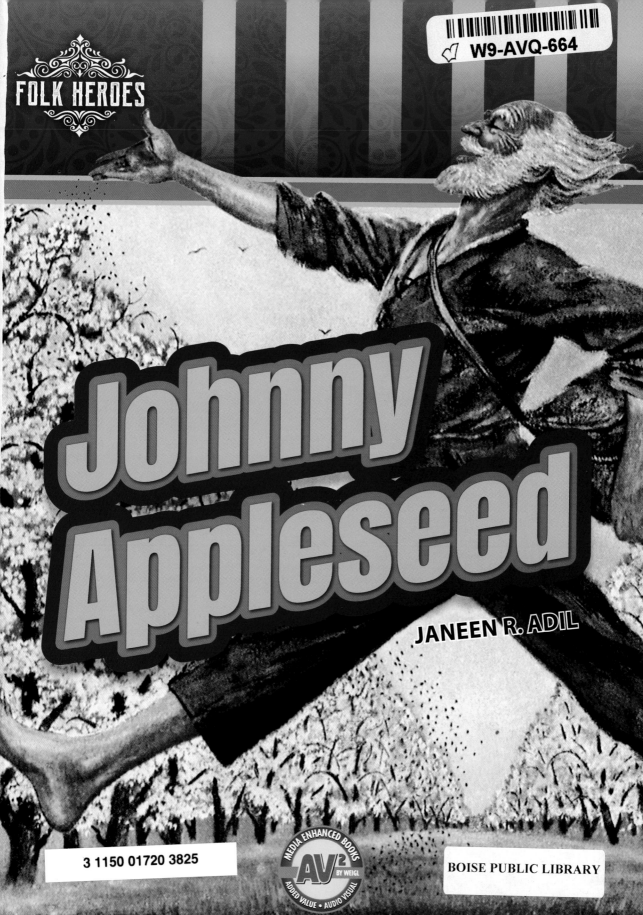

FOLK HEROES

Johnny Appleseed

JANEEN R. ADIL

MEDIA ENHANCED BOOKS
AV²
BY WEIGL
ADDED VALUE · AUDIO VISUAL

www.av2books.com

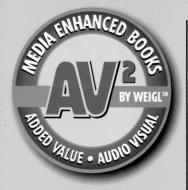

AV² provides enriched content that supplements and complements this book. Weigl's AV² books strive to create inspired learning and engage young minds in a total learning experience.

Your AV² Media Enhanced books come alive with...

Audio
Listen to sections of the book read aloud.

Key Words
Study vocabulary, and complete a matching word activity.

Video
Watch informative video clips.

Quizzes
Test your knowledge.

Go to www.av2books.com, and enter this book's unique code.

BOOK CODE

AVS75692

Embedded Weblinks
Gain additional information for research.

Slide Show
View images and captions, and prepare a presentation.

AV² by Weigl brings you media enhanced books that support active learning.

Try This!
Complete activities and hands-on experiments.

... and much, much more!

Published by AV² by Weigl
350 5th Avenue, 59th Floor
New York, NY 10118
Website: www.av2books.com

Library of Congress Cataloging-in-Publication Data
Names: Adil, Janeen R., author.
Title: Johnny Appleseed / Janeen R. Adil.
Description: New York, NY : AV2 by Weigl, [2019] | Series: Folk heroes | Includes index.
Identifiers: LCCN 2018051721 (print) | LCCN 2018052920 (ebook) | ISBN 9781489695604 (Multi User ebook) |
 ISBN 9781489695611 (Single User ebook) | ISBN 9781489695581 (hardcover: alk. paper) | ISBN 9781489695598
 (softcover: alk. paper)
Subjects: LCSH: Appleseed, Johnny, 1774-1845--Juvenile literature. | Apple growers--United States--Biography--Juvenile literature. |
 Frontier and pioneer life--Middle West--Juvenile literature.
Classification: LCC SB63.C46 (ebook) | LCC SB63.C46 A36 2019 (print) | DDC 634/.11092--dc23
LC record available at https://lccn.loc.gov/2018051721

Printed in Guangzhou, China
1 2 3 4 5 6 7 8 9 0 23 22 21 20 19

012019
130118

Project Coordinator: Heather Kissock
Art Director: Terry Paulhus

Photo Credits
Every reasonable effort has been made to trace ownership and to obtain permission to reprint copyright material. The publishers would be pleased to have any errors or omissions brought to their attention so that they may be corrected in subsequent printings.

Weigl acknowledges Alamy, Shutterstock, Bridgeman Images, and Wikimedia as its primary image suppliers for this title.

Johnny Appleseed

CONTENTS

A Peaceful Planter

John Chapman was a kind and friendly man. In his own special way, John helped the development of America by planting thousands of apple trees. John's apple trees provided the early **settlers** with food to eat.

At the time, the United States was expanding and gaining new lands. The settlers and the Native Americans were not always friendly neighbors. Often, the two groups fought over land. John respected the Native Americans and learned many skills from them. He sometimes lived with the settlers, and sometimes lived with the Native Americans, even when the two groups were at war.

John spent about 50 years traveling throughout the United States and planting apple trees.

Johnny Appleseed grew trees in what are now the states of Ohio, Pennsylvania, Kentucky, Indiana, and Illinois.

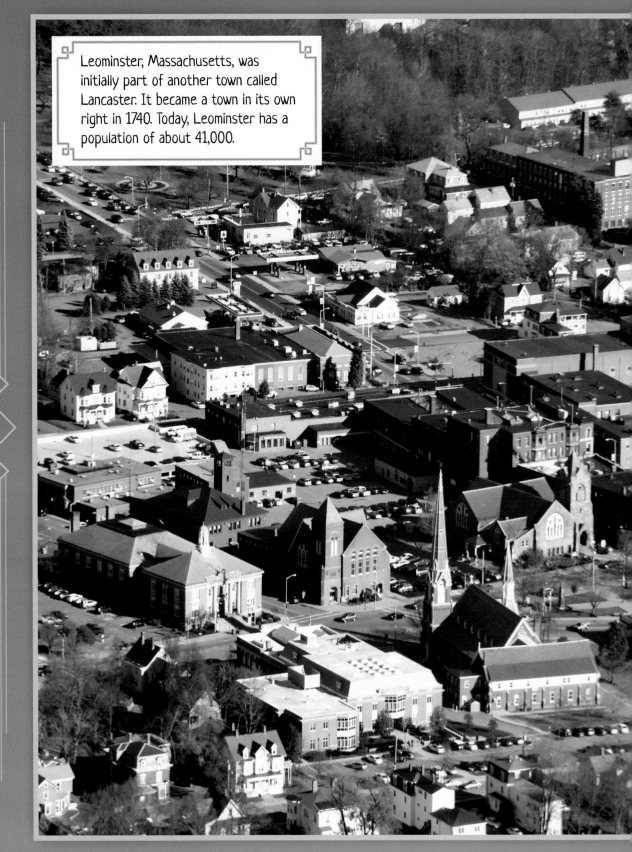

Leominster, Massachusetts, was initially part of another town called Lancaster. It became a town in its own right in 1740. Today, Leominster has a population of about 41,000.

Growing Up

J ohnny Appleseed was born on September 26, 1774, in Leominster, Massachusetts. He was still a baby when his father went to fight in the American Revolution. Johnny's mother died while his father was away. His father married again 4 years later. Their home soon became crowded with children. Johnny went into the woods to escape the noise. He found quiet and peace in the outdoors. As a young boy, he learned to love nature.

Johnny studied reading, writing, and basic mathematics at school. Most boys began to work to earn money for their families by 14 years of age. Johnny worked at a farmer's **orchard**. He likely learned how to plant and care for apple trees while working at the orchard.

Johnny's favorite book was the Bible.

Johnny Heads West

Johnny was 23 years old when he left home. He had heard stories about the rich farmlands out west and wanted to see them with his own eyes. He walked 300 miles to reach what is now the state of Pennsylvania. Johnny traveled light, bringing only some food that he carried in a bag.

Johnny traveled through all types of weather. In warmer weather, he traveled in bare feet. One day, a snowstorm hit. Johnny hid under some pine trees. During the storm, he tore strips of cloth from his coat and tied the strips around his feet and ankles. Then, he built a fire to stay warm. Johnny made **snowshoes** out of branches and kept walking.

Johnny passed many **cider mills** on his long westward journey. He noticed that brown seeds were left at the mills after the apples were crushed. Johnny gathered handfuls of the seeds and brought them with him on his travels.

Johnny Appleseed became known for always having a bag of apple seeds with him.

Apples were a staple in settlers' homes. As well as cider, they could be used to make pies, tarts, and applesauce.

Growing Apples

Johnny Appleseed planted his first apple **nursery** in 1798. The nursery was near the Allegheny River in Pennsylvania. The apple seeds grew into small trees in only a few years. When the settlers arrived, they were very happy to see Johnny's apple trees. They bought the trees to plant on their new farms.

Apples were important to the early settlers. They were eaten fresh or dried. Apples also made cider. Even the settlers' cows ate apples. Johnny's apple trees became an important part of the settlers' **legends** telling how the land was farmed.

"By **occupation** [I am] a gatherer and planter of apple seeds."

– Johnny Appleseed

The Look of a Legend

Living outdoors likely made Johnny strong and tough. One legend describes Johnny as being "straight as an arrow, slim, and wiry as a cat." His clothes were old and ragged, but they were always clean. Johnny's clothing seemed strange to many people. Johnny did not care if his clothes were in style. He just wanted to stay warm while he traveled.

Think About It

People's clothing can say a great deal about them. What do Johnny's clothes say about him? Why did Johnny wear two or three pairs of pants at the same time? Why was his hat made of cardboard? What would you wear if you lived in the 1800s? Think about why each clothing item would be important to a tree planter.

Johnny wore his hair straight and long.

Johnny wore a hat that he had made out of cardboard.

Johnny often carried the Bible on his travels.

Johnny likely used a knife to cut broken branches off his apple trees.

Johnny wore a **tunic** over an old shirt. The tunic was made out of an old coffee sack. The tunic helped keep him warm in cold weather. In warm weather, he would take it off.

Johnny rarely wore shoes. He liked to walk in bare feet.

Johnny wore two or three pairs of ragged pants to keep warm in cold weather.

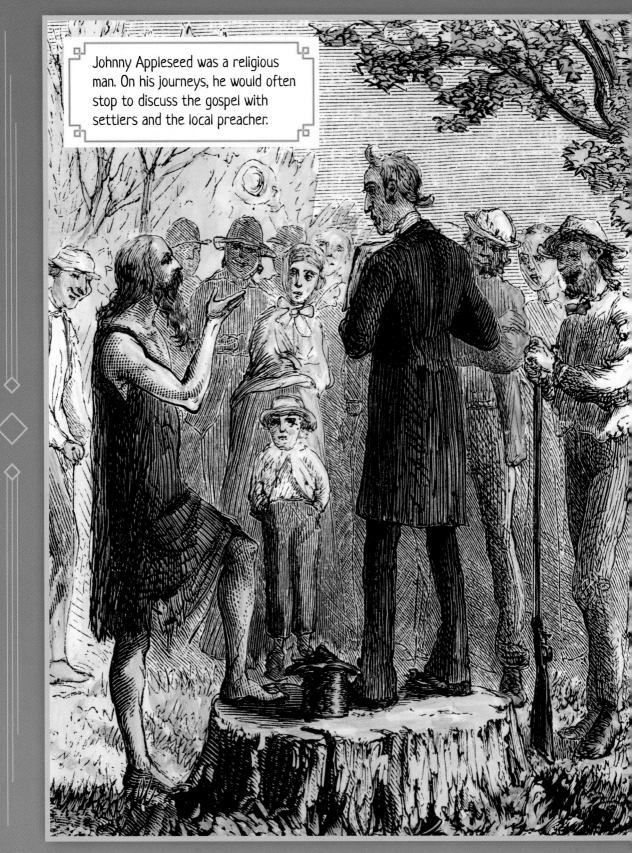

Johnny Appleseed was a religious man. On his journeys, he would often stop to discuss the gospel with settlers and the local preacher.

More Apple Trees

Johnny traveled from Pennsylvania to what are now the states of Ohio and Indiana. Every fall, Johnny gathered seeds from the cider mills in the east. Then, he would travel west again. His nurseries were planted by the time the settlers arrived. He visited each of his nurseries during spring and summer to make sure his trees were healthy and growing.

Johnny owned about 1,200 acres of apple orchards. He would travel hundreds of miles to care for each of his orchards. Along the way, he gave gifts of apple seeds to the settlers he met.

The Native Americans Johnny met on his journeys treated him with kindness. They saw that his feet were always bare and his clothes were strange. They also noticed that he did not hurt easily. The Native Americans believed that Johnny was a great **medicine man**.

Tree Tales

Johnny liked to stay with people he met during his travels. He enjoyed telling stories about his adventures. Soon, people began telling their own stories about Johnny. Some of these stories became legends. Many books, poems, movies, and songs were written about Johnny Appleseed.

In 1948, Disney released a short cartoon film about a folk hero named Johnny Appleseed. The cartoon was called "Johnny Appleseed." It featured lively songs and many colorful characters that he met in his travels.

Johnny Appleseed died in Fort Wayne, Indiana. The Johnny Appleseed Festival is held there every fall to honor him. Visiting the festival is like traveling back in time. People dress up in clothes from the 1800s. Visitors can see how Johnny Appleseed lived.

Nova, Ohio, is home to the last tree known to have been planted by Johnny. It is more than 175 years old.

Today, a statue of Johnny Appleseed stands outside the Massachusetts Visitor Center in Lancaster.

1776
Johnny's mother dies of tuberculosis, a deadly lung disease.

1780
Johnny's father marries again.

1797
Johnny begins his travels from Massachusetts to Pennsylvania.

1774

Johnny Appleseed is born in Leominster, Massachusetts, on September 26.

1798

Johnny plants his first apple nursery in Pennsylvania.

Johnny Appleseed's travels throughout the United States made him a well-known figure to settlers. Stories about his apple orchards, clothing, and kindness spread across the nation. These stories helped him become the folk hero he is today.

1801
Johnny travels to Ohio. He plants more nurseries.

1827
Johnny plants nurseries in Indiana.

1845
Some cows enter one of Johnny's nurseries. He walks 30 miles in cold, wet weather to protect his trees. He becomes ill with pneumonia. Johnny dies on March 18 in Indiana.

1812
War begins between the United States and Great Britain on June 18. Johnny continues his work during the war.

1

In which state was Johnny Appleseed born?

a) Indiana
b) Pennsylvania
c) Ohio
d) Massachusetts

2

Why did Johnny travel east every fall?

a) to go to school
b) to get apple seeds
c) to see his family
d) to buy a new ax

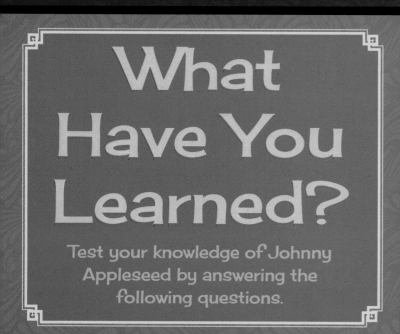

What Have You Learned?

Test your knowledge of Johnny Appleseed by answering the following questions.

3

How did Johnny usually travel?

a) by train
b) on snowshoes
c) on foot
d) by wagon

4

Where were Johnny's apple seeds planted?

a) in the woods
b) on a farm
c) in a nursery
d) near the river

5

Where did Johnny plant his first nursery?

a) Ohio
b) Pennsylvania
c) Massachusetts
d) Illinois

6

In which direction did settlers move across the United States?

a) west
b) north
c) east
d) south

7

True or False?
Johnny grew thousands of apple trees in his lifetime.

8

True or False?
Johnny liked to wear fancy, new clothes.

10

True or False?
Johnny stayed in settlers' homes.

9

True or False?
Apples were only eaten as snacks.

Map Skills

Use a map of the United States for this activity. On the map, show where Johnny was born and where he died. Label all the places that he traveled to and the dates that he was in each place. Did Johnny have to cross mountains or rivers? Was the land flat or hilly?

Show how Johnny traveled each year from east to west. Use the library and internet to research when the first settlers came to these states. How did Johnny help them start new homes and farms? Use the map below as an example to plot Johnny's journey. Start at the X, which marks Leominster.

Key Words

cider mills: factories that make a type of apple juice

legends: popular stories that cannot be proven to be true

medicine man: a person in Native American groups who cured sickness and was believed to have magic powers

nursery: a place where young plants are grown

occupation: job

orchard: a place where fruit trees grow

settlers: people who move to a new country to make their homes

snowshoes: wooden frames for walking on the snow's surface

tunic: a large shirt

Index

Log on to www.av2books.com

AV² by Weigl brings you media enhanced books that support active learning. Go to www.av2books.com, and enter the special code found on page 2 of this book. You will gain access to enriched and enhanced content that supplements and complements this book. Content includes video, audio, weblinks, quizzes, a slideshow, and activities.

AV² Online Navigation

Audio
Listen to sections of the book read aloud.

Book Pages
AV² pages directly correspond to pages in the book.

Video
Watch informative video clips.

Embedded Weblinks
Gain additional information for research.

Key Words
Study vocabulary, and complete a matching word activity.

Try This!
Complete activities and hands-on experiments.

Quizzes
Test your knowledge.

Slideshow
View images and captions, and prepare a presentation.

AV² was built to bridge the gap between print and digital. We encourage you to tell us what you like and what you want to see in the future.

Sign up to be an AV² Ambassador at www.av2books.com/ambassador.